Tiny Broadwick
The First Lady of Parachuting

Tiny Broadwick
The First Lady of Parachuting

By Elizabeth Whitley Roberson

PELICAN PUBLISHING COMPANY
Gretna 2001

*The word "Pelican" and the depiction of a pelican are trademarks
of Pelican Publishing Company, Inc., and are registered in the
U.S. Patent and Trademark Office.*

Library of Congress Cataloging-in-Publication Data

Roberson, Elizabeth Whitley.
    Tiny Broadwick : the first lady of parachuting / by Elizabeth Whitley
    Roberson
        p. cm.
    Includes bibliographical references and index.
    ISBN 1-56554-780-2 (alk. paper)
    1. Brown, Georgia Thompson, 1893-1978. 2. Skydivers—United States—
Biography. 3. Aeronautics—Records. 4. Women in aeronautics—United
States. I. Title.

TL751.B76 R63 2001
797.5'6'092—dc21
[B]

                                                            00-068207

Printed in the United States of America
Published by Pelican Publishing Company, Inc.
1000 Burmaster Street, Gretna, Louisiana 70053

Dedicated to the memory of Tiny Broadwick, whose bravery and fearlessness in demonstrating the "life preserver of the air" has saved the lives of countless pilots, and in so doing, has brought honor, not only to herself, but also to her family, her state, and her nation.

Contents

Preface

I first heard about Tiny Broadwick a few years ago, and was intrigued by the fact that as a teacher of North Carolina history, I had never seen her name in a history book. I have found in other instances that those left out of history texts are often the most interesting. Thus began my search for information about Tiny. I quickly realized that my task would be a difficult one since there has been so little written about her. Because I had numerous other commitments at the time, I had to postpone my research until recently.

My first contact was with historian T.H. Pearce of Franklin County, who knew Tiny personally and not only had information about her, but also many photographs of her. I next spoke with Lyman McLean in Tiny's hometown of Henderson, North Carolina, who had also known her very well. He shared newspaper articles and other information with me about her career as a parachutist. Additionally, I was fortunate to meet some of Tiny's relatives in Henderson. Her great-grand-daughter, Dixie Young, shared many of the family photos that have been so beneficial in producing this book.

Two other sources of information came from her friends, Maxine Hix and Father Pat McPolin of California. Maxine met Tiny in her later years, helping her become involved with various aeronautical groups. As a result, a whole new generation of people in the aeronautical industry became aware of Tiny's achievements, which made her famous again and gave her much joy during the last years of her life. Father Pat, who lives at the Ranchero Dominguez in Los Angeles, the site of the first air meet in America, knew and loved Tiny. His collection of her memorabilia, which he has displayed in his air museum, added greatly to my research.

Since Tiny's career as a parachutist was so short-lived, lasting only from 1908-1922, it has been difficult to find much information about her. Regardless, this book is the record of a remarkable woman, one whose bravery and fearlessness paved the way for so many others who have followed. She made flying much safer for the thousands of pilots of World War I until the present.

How sad it is that there is a street named for Tiny Broadwick in Los Angeles, yet there is so little knowledge of her in her own home state. I feel much richer for having learned about her and hope that she will finally receive the honor and recognition that she so richly deserves!

ELIZABETH WHITLEY ROBERSON

CHAPTER 1

Leaving Home

North Carolina was the site of the first powered airplane flight made by the Wright brothers at Kitty Hawk, North Carolina, in 1903. In 1913, only ten years later, North Carolina could also claim the first parachute jump from an airplane made by a woman, the incomparable Georgia "Tiny" Broadwick.

Her given name was Georgia Ann Thompson. She was born in 1893 on a farm in Granville County, North Carolina, the youngest of the seven daughters of George and Emma Ross Thompson. Because she weighed only three pounds when she was born, they began calling her "Tiny." Even at full maturity, she was only 4' 1" and weighed a mere 80 pounds.

Tiny's early life on the farm was one of hardship. It was difficult in those days to support such a large family, so all the children had to work long hard hours in the fields just to survive. The Thompsons raised pigs and chickens that provided a large part of their diet, but Tiny recalled that her first job was working in the tobacco fields picking worms off the tobacco leaves. With a drop in farm prices, it became harder and harder to support his family, so when Tiny was six years old, her father moved them to the little town of Henderson, North Carolina, where he could find employment in the cotton mill.

The Harriet Cotton Mill was founded in 1895 for the purpose of manufacturing and selling cotton socks and cotton print material. It was quite a large mill for that time, and when it first opened, it had two hundred four looms and supporting equipment in operation. The only problem was that its workers had to work long, hard hours for very little pay. In spite of these drawbacks however, it did provide a living for the Thompson family.

A few years after the Thompsons moved to Henderson, twelve year-old Tiny met and married William Aulsie Jacobs. One year later, she gave birth to a daughter she named Verla. When she was questioned about marrying at such a tender age, with a twinkle in her eyes she replied, "Honey, that's the way it was done down South!"

A short time after the baby's birth, Tiny's husband abandoned her. To support herself and her baby, she began working twelve-hour shifts at the cotton mill for forty cents a day. Since she was breast-feeding her baby, she would go home at ten o'clock to feed her, walk back to the mill, and return home at noon for her own dinner. She would then walk back to the mill and go home again for the baby's three o'clock feeding. All of this strain, plus working twelve- and fourteen-hour shifts in the mill, took its toll on the frail girl; she said later that she just wanted to get away from that part of the country and the numbing drudgery of mill work. Unbeknownst to her, she would have the opportunity sooner than she thought, and her life would change forever the day the Johnny J. Jones Carnival came to nearby Raleigh.

The carnival's headquarters were in Jacksonville, Florida, and it traveled by train all over the United States. Tiny had heard her co-workers talking about the carnival that would soon be coming to the state fair in Raleigh, whose main attraction featured a hot air balloon with a man parachuting from it high above the ground. To a young girl who had only known hard work and had never had a chance to be a child herself, it was a thrilling thought. Finally, she found someone who would take her to Raleigh to see this show.

The show featured Charles Broadwick, who

ascended in a free-drifting hot air balloon and then floated to earth in a parachute. His balloon, made of canvas, was ninety-two feet high and open at the bottom. He built a huge fire in a pit three feet deep, and the hot air rose into the balloon, lifting it off the ground. After his ascent high over the crowd, he slipped into a parachute that was harnessed to the bottom of the balloon and floated out into the air, lighting and smoking a cigarette on the way down. His act was to draw the crowd to all the other events at the circus, but his act was the only one Tiny had eyes for, and she stayed right by his launch site until he landed.

A *Durham Morning Herald* interview many years later included Tiny's first reaction to the sight of that balloon drop. She said, "When I seen this balloon go up, I knew that's all I ever wanted to do! I hung around till they came back to the lot where the balloon had left from and told them I wanted to join them. I was hell-bound and determined to get in that act!"

After finding Broadwick, Tiny told him of her desire to go up in the balloon, convincing him that she could do an even better job of parachuting than he had done, due to her small size. Broadwick was almost ready to agree to take Tiny along when she mentioned having a baby, and that cast a new light on the situation. He said the baby would be a hindrance to their constant moving from town to town, and therefore it would be better for her to stay at home.

Broadwick and the owner of the circus both realized however, what a drawing card this pretty, shapely girl would be for their show, so Broadwick finally agreed to talk to Tiny's mother to see if they could work things out. Her mother said, "Well, she's so young, I don't know if she should go." Broadwick assured her, however, that he would take good care of her daughter and that if she didn't succeed with her first jump, he would send her back home with enough money to support her for a year. He also agreed to send back a good portion of Tiny's salary for her baby daughter's support and future schooling. Her mother finally agreed, but only if the baby were allowed to stay at home with her. Tiny packed her few belongings and went back to Raleigh with Broadwick, where she officially joined the circus. She was on her way to a new life that would take her far from the tobacco fields and cotton mills of North Carolina. Under the tutelage of Broadwick, she changed her name, acquired an entirely new image, and began a career that took her all over the United States, making her the sweetheart of carnival crowds.

Miss Tiny Broadwick
of The Broadwicks
World's Famous Aeronauts

This is the type of balloon used by Tiny in her first jump at the North Carolina State Fair in Raleigh. (Courtesy of T.H.Pearce)

CHAPTER 2

On the Road
with Charles Broadwick

Tiny's first jump was in 1908 at the North Carolina State Fair in Raleigh. When asked what her feelings were when she first parachuted off the balloon, she said, "I tell you honey, it was the most wonderful sensation in the world! I don't think I was scared, but I was nervous." After the initial shock of leaving the ground subsided, she said that her nerves settled down and she was able to enjoy the sensation of floating on air. She found herself able to appreciate the beauty of the earth from a new perspective, and attributed her peace of mind to being in the presence of God. However, she commented that, "When I cut away from the balloon, it seemed like my heart, my tongue, and everything was coming out of my mouth!"

With that first jump, Tiny caused a moment of excitement because of her landing. She laughingly told of the event in which she had a large open field to land in, yet she somehow managed to land right in the middle of a big blackberry bush. Unable to free herself from the briars, she settled down and waited for help to arrive. Not knowing in what condition they might find her, her rescuers must have been surprised when they parted the bushes to see her berry-stained face smiling up at them! Luckily Tiny only suffered a few scratches from this fall.

With this jump, Tiny became a member of the Broadwick World Famous Aeronauts, which was booked by the circus as "an act without parallel." Broadwick capitalized on Tiny's diminutive size, her long brown curls, and her youth by dressing her like a doll, and billing her as "the Doll Girl." Tiny said in later years that she was a tomboy and hated dressing up. She said, "It burned me up having to dress like a baby doll and having that name tacked on me!" She was outfitted in ruffled bloomers with pink bows on her arms, ribbons in her long curls, and a little bonnet on her head, all of which made her look like a little child. She was also fitted with special shoes to protect her ankles from being injured when she landed on the ground. Tiny much preferred wearing boys' pants because she said that when she fell in a tree with a dress on, "all this modesty came up and you could see too much of me! I was far from being a doll, but that's the way they billed me."

Just after Tiny joined Broadwick's group, he legally adopted her as his daughter, giving her the name of Tiny Broadwick. According to family members, Tiny's father did not object to the adoption since the social mores of the day dictated that it was improper for a young girl to travel around the country alone with an older man. Broadwick began teaching her all the intricacies of parachuting from a balloon; there was much to learn about the craft if one was to survive. She learned how to fold the parachute and how to tell the exact moment she should take off for the ground. It all amounted to getting up in the air safely and getting back down again without injuring anyone.

Since she didn't have an altimeter, she had to listen closely for the drop signal, a blank fired from a pistol by Broadwick who was watching her from the ground. She also had to learn about clouds, wind, and the rigging of the all-cotton parachute. The parachute usually rose two thousand feet or higher, and if she were going to make three parachute drops from one fall, she would go up about three

Tiny with her adoptive father, Charles Broadwick. (Courtesy of Dixie Young)

thousand feet. The winds at one thousand to two thousand feet were seldom predictable, and steering the parachute was difficult, if not impossible.

The balloons were huge, containing over eleven hundred yards of a lightweight sheeting like unbleached muslin, standing ninety-two feet high and measuring fifty-six feet through the middle. They had cotton ropes in them that strung out about thirty feet from the top of the balloon to where Tiny hung on the trapeze at the bottom. It would rise with Tiny suspended under it until the air inside cooled. At this point, just as the balloon reached its maximum height, and before it cooled enough to start to fall, Tiny would release herself and float to the ground to the cheering crowds below.

Tiny learned to depend on herself to get out of unexpected difficulties. She maintained that anybody could tell her what to do on the ground, but once she was in the air, she had to work it out for herself. Although Tiny found the jumping exciting, she was always aware of the dangers involved with the sport. As careful as one might be, there was always the potential for an accident, particularly when the balloon was being inflated. Since the heat for the balloon was powered by coal oil, there was the ever-present possibility of it catching fire, endangering the people who were holding on

THE BROADWICKS
Famous French Aeronauts

Permanent Address "BILLBOARD"   CINCINNATI, OHIO

The most refined, neatest and fastest Balloons in the world.

No outside assistance.

No falling poles.

We are the inventors of the patent Ground Holding device with many other new inventions.

The public is not asked to help hold the Balloons.

Our inventions enables us to make complete ascension in 15 minutes including filling of balloon.

FEATURING

The Doll Girl, the smallest and most scientific girl aeronaut in the world.

OUR FEATURE ACTS

Six parachute drops by Doll Girl.

Balloon races between 2, 3 and 4 balloons each rider during 1, 2, 3 and 4 parachute drops.

Four parachute drop off 1 balloon by 2 people.

Six parachute drop off 1 balloon by 2 people.

Eight parachute drop off 1 balloon by 2 people.

One aeronaut riding 3 parachutes all open at the same time then cutting off with the fourth parachute, all different colors.

Shot from a cannon 3000 feet in the air doing three parachute drops, out of cannon.

Night ascensions with fireworks and parachute drop, fire works all the way up and all the way down.

We also feature all colors of parachutes.

We also feature sensational parachute, dropping three, four and five hundred feet before opening.

We can furnish every kind of Balloon act you wish from the cheapest to the largest and most sensational Balloon acts in the world.

The act that pleases and really produces every act we advertise.

Early poster advertising Broadwick's show.

to it. To lessen this danger, Broadwick developed an automatic ground support that eliminated having to hold the balloon while it was being inflated. In those days, there was no gauge to indicate when it was ready to rise. You only had your intuition to guide you.

Tiny related an incident when her balloon failed. As she began her ascension, the balloon burst. They had not noticed that the heat had scorched the outside of the balloon, weakening it so that with the combination of Tiny's weight and that of her parachute, it split open. She had only gotten about two hundred feet off the ground when it split, and unfortunately, she didn't have enough time to cut loose. She fell ten or twelve feet, landing on the carnival tent, hitting the ropes that supported it. Upon impact, the balloon collapsed, tearing down the tent. Luckily, Tiny was not injured in the fall.

Another narrow escape occurred during a flight when she realized that the wind was taking her toward two large buildings. She tried to maneuver a landing on the roof of one of them, but the wind was taking her between the two. She said she knew if she went down between the buildings, there would be nothing to hold her up, and it would be a dead drop from the top down. She said, "I was so scared that I just barely made it over on the other roof, and if there hadn't been one of those cement walls up there to hold me, I would have fallen."

She explained her method of determining during her ascent how and where she would gauge her landing. On the way up, she would pick out the location of trees because it was safer to land in a tree than on top of a building. She explained, "Coming down, you can steer the parachute by raising or lowering the sides of the wooden ring, which holds the seat." On one of her jumps, the first two sections of the parachute did not open and she landed on a windmill; however, her parachute didn't catch on the vanes of the mill, so she fell face-down on the ground. Fortunately, she suffered only a broken arm, a dislocated shoulder, and a sprained ankle.

Tiny also described landing on a train just as it was leaving the station, but the engineer saw her coming and put on the brakes. Just as the train came to a stop, Tiny hit the rear end of it and her right elbow went through a coach window, dislocating her shoulder. She later said that she wasn't hurt seriously, but the passengers in that car sure were surprised!

One of her funniest landings occurred in a cemetery just as a young girl was walking by. The sight of the white figure floating to the ground in among the tombstones scared the girl almost to death. She ran away screaming, thinking Tiny was an angel descending from Heaven!

Tiny's performances drew large crowds to the circus, but unfortunately, she was not reaping the benefits of the money she was generating. She had joined the circus in order to make a living for herself and her daughter, but Broadwick was a poor manager of the money they made. Although Tiny was supposed to get two hundred fifty dollars a week plus traveling expenses, at times she was accepting Coca-Colas and sandwich money as her pay. In spite of this, she said, "I was kid enough to enjoy it!" She loved the excitement of the throngs of people who gathered to watch her perform and loved to hear their applause as she floated gracefully down to earth. She reveled in their devotion to her, waiting sometimes for hours until the wind was just right for the balloon to make its ascension.

In an interview with Kenneth Leish, Tiny was asked if she felt she was taking tremendous chances every day. She responded, "No, I didn't. I knew I was good, that I was doing something that I knew something about, something that I wanted to do, and I loved it." Like many people in the stunt world, Tiny sometimes had premonitions of danger at work. She refused to go up in a balloon if these feelings were particularly strong. On one occasion she had a premonition, but since there

At times, the only pay Tiny received for her spectacular jumps was a glass of Coca-Cola! (Courtesy of Dixie Young)

was no one else to take her place, she felt obligated to go anyway. Unbeknownst to her, someone had kicked a knife on the chute, cutting the rope in half; as she took off from the ground, she and the parachute dropped away from the balloon. It gave her quite a scare, but luckily she was not hurt.

Tiny's aerial act had six different parts. She said, "Sometimes we'd make a double balloon ascent. Whoever was working with us would do two parachutes, and I would do four." Tiny described the parachutes as being red, white, and blue. She would fall first with the red, then the white, and finally the blue, always ending with the flag hanging on the bottom of the trapeze on which she was riding. She said it was always an interesting point—to see a flag flying down from the trapeze, with her sitting on the trapeze beside it.

Tiny also explained how they made the show more exciting. She said that she would do several back jumps on the parachute and a few little stunts on the trapeze, but nothing too spectacular. Sometimes she said they used fireworks, but she was always afraid of her clothes catching fire. She said, "When you left the balloon, you had to ignite your flares, and then in the drop, there was always the danger of setting your parachute and your clothes on fire." Because the flares hung out only about two feet on each side of the parachute, the danger of fire was ever present as the parachute began its descent. Fortunately, Tiny was never injured while executing this maneuver.

Tiny cited several reasons why the Broadwick show was better than most. One reason, she said, was the fact that their act was neat and fast, with complete balloon ascension in only fifteen minutes. This included filling the balloon and getting it up in the air. She said, "Then you'd be back on the ground in fifteen or twenty minutes, unless the weather would delay it." They could ascend so fast because of their automatic ground support that necessitated having fifteen people to hold the balloon down.

To keep the balloon from falling when the wind was blowing, they had two poles on each side that would automatically telescope when they were ready to ascend, releasing the cord through the top of the balloon. Tiny said, "That's what made our act so safe and fast, and so much more advanced than the others."

When asked how many jumps she performed a day, Tiny said, "At the carnivals, you'd do one in the daytime and then one in the evening. We didn't go in for double parachute jumps at night." She said that the nighttime jumps were made more spectacular by using torches and flares. Tiny usually made only six jumps a week, but was paid twenty-five dollars extra if she made more than that.

Broadwick's World Famous Aeronauts performed from the Atlantic to the Pacific and from Canada to Mexico. All this time, Tiny was becoming something of a national figure. One of the first shows in which she was featured was in 1908 at the Florida Ostrich Farm and Zoo in Jacksonville, where people gathered on Sundays for outstanding feats of skydiving and acrobatics. Other acts included ostrich races and song and dance routines. The most spectacular act however, was that of the Broadwicks.

Newspaper accounts described Tiny as the most daring female aeronaut ever seen in that city, and in spite of her frail size, she performed like a veteran. Although the exhibition featured other acts, the papers reported that Tiny's was the greatest feature of the program. They described her act as consisting of a triple parachute drop. She ascended in the balloon to a height of several thousand feet and then began three successive parachute drops. She jumped from the balloon, leaving two parachutes floating in the air several thousand feet from the ground and ended up clinging to the third parachute, returning to the ground. This was a dangerous maneuver, and the reporter covering the event said that it was always a relief to the spectators when they saw her safely descending, clinging to the third parachute.

MISS TINY BROADWICK
World's Most Daring Aviatrice-Parachutist

Amazing, Startling, Nerve-Tingling Leap From Military Aeroplane 8,000 Feet in the Sky, Landing Within a Few Feet of a Selected Spot. (Using Chas. Broadwick's Patent Safety Pack Vest.)

MOST SENSATIONAL ACT STAGED DURING CHICAGO AND BUFFALO'S GREAT 1913 WATER CARNIVAL AND MOTOR BOAT CHAMPIONSHIPS

RAIN OR SHINE WIND OR CALM
ONLY ACT OF THE KIND
A TINY CHANCE-TAKING SLIP OF A GIRL IN THE ONE FEAT REQUIRING THE MAXIMUM OF NERVE SKILL AND DARING

LINCOLN BEACHEY, INC., WESTMINSTER BLDG., CHICAGO

In a performance there in January 1909, she caused a lot of excitement when it was thought she would surely be killed. As Broadwick was preparing the balloon for its trip skyward, the wind reversed its course quite abruptly, and it was all he could do to keep it from being ignited by the flames from the ground furnace. Finally, the balloon was filled and the guy ropes were cut, carrying the three parachutes and Tiny dangling from a crossbar. The balloon kept rising until it reached a height of twenty-five hundred feet when it stopped, having encountered a vacuum. Broadwick knew how dangerous this was, and he had to act quickly. He fired his pistol twice as a signal to drop and then fired it again to instruct Tiny to drop with the two last parachutes attached to the balloon.

Suddenly, the crowd saw a long white object drop like a torpedo, and when it opened, they saw the little aeronaut safely descending to the ground. Since she realized that the distance was too short to allow a double drop, she did a single; however, she landed on a picket fence that badly lacerated her feet. With great effort, suffering excruciating pain, she managed to find her way back to the Ostrich Farm. The people at the resort saw Tiny's safe landing; however, people in other parts of the city saw the parachute dangling from the bottom of the balloon and thought she was still attached as the balloon went up in clouds of smoke and gas. This close call terrified Broadwick, since four years earlier his wife, Maud, was killed in a similar accident when she fell five hundred feet from a balloon while performing at Buena Vista Park in Anderson, South Carolina.

Since much of the jumping Tiny did in Florida was near water, she had to learn how to handle her parachute if she should land in it. Those first parachutes were made of cotton, and soaked up water very quickly. She said, "If you didn't know how to throw a parachute when going in the water, you would be in trouble. Lots of people have drowned that way, even in later years." Tiny must have quickly mastered the skill of landing in water since it was reported that sometimes she would land in the river at least three times a week!

There was not only danger from falling in the water, but other hazards often caused Tiny some anxious moments. Once she landed on some high-tension wires, burning the parachute from her body. On another occasion, she sprained her ankle when she fell into some telephone wires. It is amazing that with the number of jumps she made, she managed to escape serious injury.

CHAPTER 3

In the Air with Glenn Martin

In 1910, the world's first International Aviation Meet was held at Dominguez Field in Los Angeles. It was such a success that it was held there again in 1911, the year Broadwick scheduled a show in that city. He had heard about the meet and agreed to participate. Tiny went up in the balloon, but when a second current hit her, the balloon carried her far away from where it was launched. One of the pilots who was also participating in the meet flew after Tiny and landed on the field where she had descended. He flew her back to the grandstand to see the rest of the competition. This was her first airplane ride and she loved it!

The year 1912 marked a turning point in Tiny's

Tiny's balloon at Dominguez Field in 1912. (Courtesy of Dixie Young)

career. She and Broadwick had returned to Los Angeles to participate in the third meet at Dominguez Field. It was here that she would meet Glenn L. Martin, a young aviator who had achieved fame as an outstanding "barnstormer."

Martin was born in 1886 in Macksburg, Iowa, the son of a hardware salesman. Working with his father and being surrounded by farming equipment helped him develop mechanical skills that would benefit him in his later endeavors. He often daydreamed about the possibility of flight, and after the Wright brothers flew their plane at Kitty Hawk in 1903, Glenn dreamed of building and flying his own plane.

In 1907, Glenn's family moved to Santa Ana, California, where he met Charles Willard, who would later go into business with him. After settling into the new home, Glenn began building gliders that he tried out on the nearby hills. After building three of them, he decided to construct an airplane. Finally, in 1908, with his mother's support and the help of several men he had met, the plane was completed. Unfortunately, his first test was not successful, and the plane was demolished before it ever left the ground. After this failed attempt, Glenn's father tried to discourage him from building another plane, but Glenn's mother totally supported her son's dream of flying and helped him build another plane, even at the cost of destroying her own marriage.

Glenn wrote to the Wright brothers in Ohio, asking for permission to build a pusher-type biplane under their patents, which they readily agreed to do. Little did he know that he and Orville would work together in the years to come. With endorsement from Orville, Glenn and his mother looked for a place for him to build the plane. They found an abandoned church that they rented for twelve dollars a month. Glenn read everything he could find about flying machines, and in the summer of 1909, without the benefit of technical education or flight instruction, he built and flew his first airplane.

He and his fellow workers pushed the plane by hand for a distance of four miles to the field where it would be tested. The test proved a success; Glenn flew one hundred feet in twelve seconds at an altitude of eight feet. It wasn't a spectacular flight, but it demonstrated that his design could indeed fly.

As he continued flying, he learned more and more about how to control the aircraft and other logistics of the art of flight. After he was able to replace the thirty horsepower engine with a seventy horsepower, he could fly higher and longer. His first advertised exhibition took place in an Irvine, California, bean field on November 21,

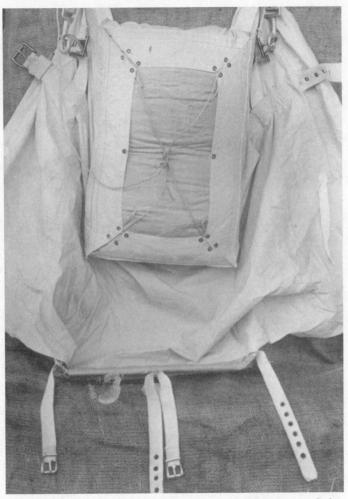

A close-up view of the Broadwick coat pack. (Courtesy of the National Air and Space Museum, Smithsonian Institution, Photo No. 2000-1373)

Tiny as seen after her jump at the Dominguez Air Meet in 1912. (Courtesy of the National Air and Space Museum, Smithsonian Institution, Photo No. 2000-1368)

Glenn Martin and Glenn Curtiss at the First Professional Air Meet at Dominguez Ranchero near Compton, California, 1910. (Courtesy of Dixie Young)

Tiny's first landing from an airplane. (Courtesy of T.H. Pearce)

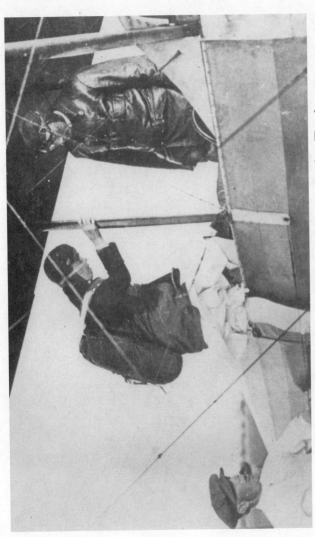

Griffith Field in Los Angeles on June 21, 1913. On this day, Tiny became the first female to jump from a plane in a parachute. (Courtesy of the National Air and Space Museum, Smithsonian Institution, Photo No. 77-715)

1910, which drew large numbers of spectators, many of whom had once predicted he would never get off the ground!

In January 1910, he attended the first professional air meet held in the United States at Dominguez Ranchero near Compton, California. Pioneer aviators first flew on the Dominguez Hills and parachutists jumped from balloons. This event attracted such famed pilots as Glenn Curtiss and Louis Paulthon, the famed French pilot who flew seventy-five miles in one hour and fifty-eight minutes.

When the second Dominguez Meet was held in December 1911, Glenn was a participant, and though he didn't earn much money in the competition, he made some valuable contacts with people who would later help him achieve his goal of building airplanes on a large scale. Tiny Broadwick jumped from her parachute at this second air meet, but it was at the third meet in 1912 that she caught Martin's eye.

At the Third Dominguez Air Meet, Glenn introduced his Model Twelve plane with a sixty horsepower Hall-Scott engine. He later added a pontoon to this plane and began taking off at Balboa Bay. He was constantly competing with Glenn Curtiss to build bigger and better planes, and on the morning of May 10, 1912, he set a record for over-water flight. He was on a barnstorming tour when he saw a pretty girl by the

Broadwick gives Tiny her last minute instructions as she prepares to go up in an army plane to demonstrate his parachute. Static line which she later cut is shown attached to her parachute. (Courtesy of T.H. Pearce)

Tiny and Glenn Martin with reporter Grace Wilcox before takeoff at Griffith Park. (Courtesy of Dixie Young)

name of Tiny Broadwick in a hot air balloon exhibition. He watched excitedly as her balloon reached a predetermined altitude, at which time she jumped from the basket and began falling toward the ground with her parachute opening just in time to drop her safely to the ground.

After watching this act and seeing the effect it had on the crowds, Glenn saw that it could add sparkle to his own act of exhibition and precision flying. He saw the potential this charming girl had in bringing out cash customers, so he introduced himself to Tiny and her father and asked Tiny if she would parachute from his plane. Much to his surprise, without any hesitation, she said yes. This event marked a whole new chapter in Tiny's career, and ultimately gave her a place in history as the first woman to drop from an airplane.

Tiny's first jump from Martin's plane was on June 21, 1913. The six-pound silk parachute she used was one developed by Broadwick that he advertised as the "Patent Safety Pack Vest." It looked like a knapsack attached to a snug-fitting canvas jacket to which harness straps were stitched. A string was fastened to the fuselage of the plane and then woven through the canvas covering so that when the wearer fell from the plane, the covering would be ripped off, leaving the parachute free to fill.

Later however, the pack was designed to be operated manually by the parachutist pulling the release cord and breaking the strings holding the pack closed. Tiny was suspended from a trap seat just behind the wing outside the cockpit, and the parachute was placed on a shelf above it. A funnel arrangement was placed in front of her to prevent the backwash from the propeller from taking her breath. Glenn took the plane up to two thousand feet, at which time Tiny released the lever alongside the seat, allowing the seat to drop out from under her.

The site of the first flight with Martin was in Los Angeles, in what is now part of the Los Angeles Zoo in Griffith Park. On the morning of the flight, there were many news reporters gathered there to watch this exciting event. Two of the reporters, Grace Wilcox and Bonnie Glessner, wrote the following articles for their respective newspapers after they accompanied Tiny and Martin on that eventful day:

I experienced yesterday a sensation and beheld a sight the like of which has never been experienced and seen before by a woman who realized and knew what was happening. From the top side of an aeroplane, looking down, I watched a young girl with a life pack on her back, slip over the side of the airship, down and always down to earth—twelve hundred feet below her—while I was always above.

Many have seen this same girl from the ground as with their eyes cast heavenward and their necks twisted backward they watched her come to earth.

It is a vastly different thing to watch this thing happen

*from the air than from the earth! Seldom, indeed, is it
given to anyone to see the flight of a human body through
the air, while the watching eyes are looking earthward
instead of skyward.*

*Tiny Broadwick yesterday afternoon crossed the great
divide between the clouds and the earth—and I was
always watching her from above! With Glenn Martin in
his aeroplane and Tiny Broadwick trying out her
father's safety device, I flew for the first time into the
land peopled only by the birds and the drifting clouds—
the land undiscovered and almost unexplored—the
land which is not land, but the air. And the most mar-
velous thing about that flight was the descent of Tiny
Broadwick, who jerked herself loose from the aircraft
and sailed down the sunbeams to earth.*

*Out at Griffith Park yesterday, big-souled, fearless
men chatted lightly enough about the Martin Aeroplane.
Here a crowd of boys talked about "her" in breathless
whispers. "Now you by careful when you come down—
there's quite a stiff wind this afternoon," said Mr.
Broadwick to his daughter, Miss Tiny, and she with a
saucy little toss of the head, replied, "Oh, I guess a little
wind isn't going to hurt anything!"*

*Then there was a bit of a scurry and hustle and
Glenn Martin was seen to climb aboard his "ship" and
with a nod and a wave of the hand he whirled up and
away on his trial flight. "I wish I could go now—I just
love to drop," said little Tiny. The "drop," which this slip
of a girl mentioned so nonchalantly, is a drop something
more than a thousand feet in the parachute invented by
her father. Gowned in a dark red costume, with a tight,*

cowled cap over her brown hair, with her brown eyes sparkling and a gay smile, Tiny Broadwick watched Glenn Martin as he circled about the camp in the air and wished for the moment when she might drop through that space to the ground.

Tiny Broadwick is absolutely unafraid. Dropping from an aeroplane twelve hundred feet in the air means no more to her than an automobile ride to most girls. In fact, she confided to me yesterday that she is a bit nervous when driving in a machine in the traffic downtown, but she loves the sensation of dropping in a parachute. She is attractive and unspoiled, gentle and lovable, and is idolized by her father, who straps her into the safety device and watches every movement from the time she leaves the ground until she once more reaches it.

At last Mr. Broadwick said, "The five-minute bell, Tiny." Mr. Martin gave me a warm cap and goggles and somebody else wrapped me in a comfortable leather coat, little Tiny in her red garments was fastened into her device, and in three minutes, we were seated in the machine. And today I know how a bird feels when it flies high over the world of men. Up into the cloudless sky, flying straight over the mountains, leaving the kindly earth and its cares and joys, its cities, villages, rivers, valleys, and homes far below—straight into the very heart of the great adventure!

For a moment I forgot the little girl who was so soon to leave that purring, solid body which was bearing up, up, always up. Then Tiny touched me on the shoulder. Not a word was spoken, as I saw her suddenly slip over the side of the airship, not a jar of the machine as she left the side and swayed a dizzy second between heaven and earth and then was lost to view.

Martin's plane was equipped with pontoons for a water landing. Tiny is shown in the trap seat from which she would be the first woman to make a water jump from an airplane. (Courtesy of Dixie Young)

Suddenly I became conscious of a tightening of the muscles around my throat; a cold chill flashed like an electric current through my body, and in a sickening second I realized that the little girl was gone. Where? I looked at Glenn Martin sitting there so calmly guiding his craft, looking apparently into space, and it seemed that the gladness of the afternoon was a horrible nightmare. I could not see that little girl—that bright scarlet figure, the shining eyes and smiling lips. Where was she?

Then Glenn pointed and far away, circling like a great red, white, and blue parasol, I saw the childlike figure of little Tiny swinging through space, lightly poised as a butterfly on a flower. Ever nearer and nearer she came to earth—with the beautiful parasol over her—nearer and nearer until I saw her touch the ground and saw her friends around her. The greatest of great adventures was over!   —GRACE WILCOX

Bonnie Glessner, a reporter for the *Los Angeles Times*, also accompanied Martin and Tiny on the flight, and her reaction to the experience appeared in the February 10, 1914, edition of the paper:

I may never be a real angel, but if as we are told, heaven lies just beyond the blue of the "inverted bowl," then I have been a whole lot nearer to heaven than a number of people I might mention.

Yesterday, Miss Tiny Broadwick and I went for a little aerial jaunt with Glenn Martin in his newest biplane, and while we only went heavenward a bit over one thousand

feet, I feel that I can at any time safely qualify as a near-angel, while if she should ever need it, I am ready to vouch for Mistress Tiny's being a sure-enough angel. For, as I watched with thickly beating heart, this nervy little girl stepped calmly over the edge of the aeroplane a thousand feet in the air, and with a brave little smile, plunged earthward.

For actual courage I do not believe anything could be found to equal that displayed by the girl who yesterday wrote a new chapter in aviation in her demonstration of the safety vest just invented by Glenn Martin. Wearing the vest tightly strapped about her she climbed over the side of the aeroplane while we continued flying at the rate of close to eighty miles an hour, and at a signal from Martin, she dropped from our sight. Then with a mighty swoop the aircraft circled down to the level of the parachute and its fearless burden and I drew a mighty sigh of relief as I saw the little lady drifting safely away to the earth, which just then seemed a long way down.

The whole action occupied but a few heart-breaking seconds, yet there, speeding between earth and heaven, those seconds were filled with life and death. Just a little miscalculation and that slip of a girl would not reach the ground in safety. If the parachute should not open as planned—a thousand terrible possibilities swept through my mind as I watched her preparations with a fascination that dulled every other sense.

Her cheeks were crimson with the stiff wind that was blowing in our faces, and from each corner of her mouth a little drawn line showed that even though she is accustomed *to parachute work, she realized the gravity of this new venture. Yet with smiling eyes she waited for the signal from Martin.*

When she was ready to drop, Martin touched my shoulder. I faced about and turned my eyes on the face of the child. She was clambering over the side of the machine as though it were stationary. Once over she clung tenaciously, her eyes fixed on Martin, who was just then looking down over the side of the aeroplane. The signal came while he watched below. Just the slight movement of his hand but the girl understood and her lips formed a "goodbye" which I sensed rather than heard. Smiling at me, she stepped off into space, not even a tremor of the machine showing she was gone.

We began our downward flight, circling about the parachute and Mistress Tiny, who would appear to be swept by us one moment and then to dart upward the next.
           —BONNIE GLESSNER

Tiny later described her own feelings about that day. She said, "I wasn't worried about jumping that day because it was so much simpler in an airplane than it was in the hot air balloon." She explained that you had very little control in a balloon because you had to travel the way the wind carried you, but in an airplane you could pick your landing spot. She said, "It was a thrill knowing I could drop without having to look out for trees, telephone wires, churches, and steeples."

Tiny was also thrilled that so far, no one had ever jumped from an airplane and she was going to be the first to accomplish such a feat. On that first flight they went up about one thousand feet with the plane going about seventy miles per hour, at which time she jumped. She was seated out front on the plane right beside Martin on the wing. When she was ready to go, she reached over and released a stick that let her drop. There was nothing to fly around and get in the way. She said, "I went straight down, my parachute opened beautifully, and I landed wonderfully." Tiny was proud of not only having been the first woman to make such a jump, but also of landing on her feet!

With all this publicity, Tiny and Martin were in great demand all over the country. Broadwick neglected securing a patent on his chute however, and never realized any of the huge profits it would eventually generate.

The same year as the jump in Los Angeles, they went to Chicago for the Perry Victory Centennial Celebration where Tiny achieved another first by jumping from a hydroplane and landing in Lake Michigan. In preparation for this flight, Martin had to equip his plane with pontoons for the water landing. He also had to build a special funnel in front of Tiny's trap seat to keep the oil from the engine from splattering in her face.

Tiny jumped from the plane carrying a wreath, which she was to present to Governor Dunn of Illinois. She landed in the cold water of Lake Michigan where she was picked up by a small boat and carried to shore. Soaking wet and chilled to the bone, she made a teeth-chattering presentation of a soggy bouquet to the mayor. But with this jump, she became the first person to make a parachute jump from outside of a hydroplane and the first woman to make a water jump from an airplane.

After her jump, a tall, serious-looking gentleman from Dayton, Ohio, came up to her. It was none other than Wilbur Wright! Tiny said, "He stuck out his hand and I stuck out mine and he said, 'You're awful small to do that.' I just said, 'Thank you.' I was too scared to say anything else. I had once been to his bicycle shop in Dayton when I was traveling with the circus. Now I wish I had had the courage to talk to him more!"

After her first jump from Martin's plane, they were in great demand all over the country, and in April 1914 they were asked to participate in the ground-breaking ceremonies of the World's Greatest Speedway in Pomona, California. The officials wanted a spectacular show so Glenn staged one complete with air races, demonstrations of air to ground wireless communications, an attempt by himself to break the world's altitude record, and topped it all off with parachute drops by Tiny Broadwick. The event was a great success. Sometime around Christmas of that year they were hired to drop promotion slips over Los Angeles for various businesses. They dropped three thousand envelopes, each containing a coupon worth many times its weight in gold. The presents were gifts to the people of Los Angeles from the *Tribune* and the *Express* as well as hundreds of merchants. The coupons, when presented at the business office of either newspaper, entitled the holder to an order for that present. The gifts covered everything from shoes to a payment on a piece of real estate. When they landed, a friend remarked to Tiny, "You look cold." She answered, "Oh, I'm warm now. I was cold for a while but I got warmed up. I've made many flights with Mr. Martin but never one that was more beautiful or gratifying than today's. Los Angeles looked like a dream city to us, way up there in the clouds!"

After the event, the following article appeared in the *Express*:

At 2:15 this afternoon a tiny speck was propelled into the clearer atmosphere from the haze hanging over the northern boundary of Los Angeles city. It veered toward the west, turned, speeded eastward and again turning, darted in a straight line toward a point a mile or more high and immediately above the center of the city. It grew larger every passing second and tens of thousands of people gazing upward discerned the outlines of the latest type of aeroplane.

The aerial craft was manned by Glenn Martin, its owner, and Miss Tiny Broadwick, his assistant. It was loaded with a cargo of one hundred and seventy-five pounds of gifts and souvenirs for the citizens of Los

Angeles—the greetings of the Express and the Tribune and of the merchants of the city to a multitude.

Thousands began scanning the skies for a glimpse of the modern Santa Claus and his modern conveyance, long before the time scheduled for the start at the hangar in Griffith Park, which was 2:12 p.m. As that hour approached, work was generally suspended on the new skyscrapers going up in the downtown section and virtually every window in the office buildings and hotels was filled with watchers. The rush of late Christmas shopping came to a standstill while thousands emerged from the stores to join other thousands in the streets and all eyes were turned upward.

Martin's first appearance from the north was at 2:15 and the message "Here he comes" was flashed over the city by telephone, shouts, and the sight of men, women, and children with their heads thrown back waiting expectantly for the shower of gift orders and the souvenir edition of the city's favorite newspapers that had previously announced the great event.

Many hundreds of the orders and newspapers were tossed from the aeroplane by Miss Broadwick during the passage toward the business district, but the most generous distribution was reserved for the center of the city's population.

Aviator Martin made careful calculations before his ascent. They showed that the gift orders, contained in envelopes, would descend at the rate of six and a half feet per second and that the souvenir newspaper would travel five feet in the same brief space of time. His calculations

Tiny and Glenn Martin as they prepare to drop gift coupons over the city of Los Angeles, 1914. (Courtesy of T.H. Pearce)

also showed that he must fly at a height of approximately six thousand feet and that the gifts and souvenirs must leave the aeroplane above a point two miles distant from the place where he wanted them to alight. Therefore, the messages picked up in the business section today were tossed from the aerial craft by Miss Broadwick at a point more than a mile above the vicinity of Main and Jefferson Streets.

The scramble for the gift orders and souvenirs was unlike anything that has been witnessed in any city in the world! People of all classes joined in a general stampede in the direction of every descending object while the more agile leaped high in the air and in many cases grasped the prizes before they could reach the outstretched hands of others.

Hundreds of the gifts from the clouds fell on the roofs of buildings in the business district and were gathered up by lucky persons who had sought these vantage points to watch the flight. The souvenir Expresses and Tribunes were apparently as highly prized as were the gift orders. They were the first aerial newspapers ever published and they contained the greetings of Los Angeles merchants to the citizens, the first ever delivered from "Cloudland."

As quickly as the envelopes containing the gift orders were torn open, the finders hurried to the office of the Express and the Tribune to receive a verification of the message. At one time, it was estimated that five thousand persons were in front of the newspaper building, each bearing an order for a Christmas present.

The flight of the modern Santa Claus and his pretty

companion occupied about 30 minutes. The aeroplane left the hangar at Griffith Park at 2:12 and descent was made at 2:45. The craft carried a weight of 416 pounds: the aviator 147 pounds, Miss Broadwick 94 pounds, and the gifts and souvenirs 175 pounds.

Tiny after her jump for the United States Army officials at San Diego's North Island, 1914. (Courtesy of the National Air and Space Museum, Smithsonian Institution, Photo No. 2000-1369)

CHAPTER 4

The Life Preserver
of the Air

By 1914, the United States Government had a small fleet of airplanes in service; however, some of them were not very safe to operate and many pilots perished with their planes when they crashed. The officials recognized the fact that some sort of escape for the pilot would be helpful, but they were reluctant to outfit pilots with parachutes since they said it would be too much of a temptation for the pilot to abandon his aircraft if he thought anything was wrong. At any rate, the time was ripe that day in 1914 when Tiny demonstrated the ability to abandon a plane should the need arise.

Wearing Broadwick's backpack, Tiny went aloft at San Diego's North Island with First Lieutenant

Walter R. Taliaferro as pilot. Her demonstration that day consisted of four jumps. The first three were static-line activated, where the weight of her body pulled taut a line attached to the aircraft that would automatically open the parachute. She had already completed three successful jumps when on the fourth, her static line became entangled in the tail assembly of the plane. Her frail body was whipped back and forth by the wind, and she was unable to get back into the plane or to descend to the ground. She didn't panic, however, and quickly cut off all but a short length of the static line, which she pulled by hand, freeing the shroud lines that opened the parachute. This would later be called a "ripcord," and she was the first person ever to make a premeditated "free fall" descent. This meant that a person leaving an airplane no longer needed a line attached to the plane to open his chute. Tiny's demonstration that day proved that a pilot could safely bail out of an airplane should the need arise. They called this parachute "the life preserver of the air."

General Scriven later said that Tiny's demonstration that day was the most daring achievement he had ever seen. The day after this event, the following article appeared in the *San Diego Union*:

> As the result of a flight by First Lieutenant Walter R. Taliaferro at San Diego, Brigadier General George P. Scriven, chief signal officer, USA, has recommended the

purchase of a number of parachutes to be used as life pre-
servers on army aeroplanes. On the occasion of General
Scriven's inspection of the San Diego station, a young
lady, the daughter of the inventor of the new parachute,
dropped with ease a distance of twelve hundred feet from
Lt. Taliaferro's aeroplane. General Scriven is very much
impressed with the merits of the new parachute and
thinks it is possible that it will become as much a part of
the equipment of an aeroplane as the regulation life pre-
servers are of a ship. At least, he thinks that the inven-
tion is of sufficient merit to be given a thorough test by
the government.

It wasn't until World War I began however,
before the government seriously considered
using parachutes. It was then they saw how valuable the parachute would be for pilots flying in
combat.

During World War I, Tiny and her foster father,
Charles Broadwick, went their separate ways. It
was due in part to his legal and financial troubles.
It also became harder and harder to book their
exhibitions since the novelty of flight had begun
to wane, and the crowds of people who once
attended the shows were no longer willing to pay
to see them perform. There's no record of Tiny
and Broadwick staying in touch with one another
through the ensuing years, and Charles
Broadwick died in 1943 in a veterans hospital in
California.

Tiny after her separation from Broadwick. (Courtesy of Dixie Young)

In 1912, Tiny tried to begin a normal life by marrying a schooner master named Andrew Olsen. Unfortunately, he was at sea months at a time, leaving Tiny alone at home. She later said that it was terribly hard for her to settle down since she had so much pep and energy and she grew lonesome for the excitement of parachuting. It is not known what happened to Olsen—whether he died at sea or whether he and Tiny separated—but she was jumping regularly again in 1913.

In 1916, Tiny met and married Harry Brown, a man who helped pioneer the Greyhound Bus Company line from Los Angeles, California, to Salt Lake City, Utah. She retired from jumping again because he did not approve of her parachuting out of airplanes. Her retirement lasted for four years, but in 1920, she resumed her work with Glenn Martin. Her marriage to Brown also ended in heartbreak because he deserted her and never returned.

Finally in 1922, after fourteen years of parachuting and more than one thousand jumps, she announced her retirement. Her final jump was from the Curtis-Jenny biplane, piloted by Clyde Pangborn, a famous stunt pilot who made the first nonstop flight across the Pacific Ocean in 1931. Tiny was reluctant to give up jumping, however, because she once said, "I breathe so much better

Just before going up for her last jump in 1922, she is shown here with Clyde Pangborne, a famed pioneer of aviation, and the mayor of Los Angeles.
(Courtesy of T.H. Pearce)

up there when I jump, and I'm getting so I don't like to breathe on earth."

Glenn Martin went on to become an outstanding barnstorming pilot, and he used his experience to develop several successful types of military aircraft, establishing himself as one of the leading military airplane manufacturers of the United States. He founded the Glenn L. Martin Aircraft Company, which produced greats in the business such as William Boeing, Donald Douglas, Lawrence Bell, and James S. McDonnell. His company later produced the Titan ballistic missiles for the United States Army.

CHAPTER 5

The First Lady
of Parachuting

Since Tiny had left home when she was so
young, she had received little or no education,
and when her husband abandoned her, the only
job she could find was that of a companion-house-
keeper for elderly people. However, with the out-
break of World War II, Tiny found employment at
Rohr Aircraft Company, turning out aircraft parts.
This kept her in close touch with Glenn Martin,
with whom she had spent so many happy hours.

During the war years, she was asked to talk to
some of the young paratroopers about her experi-
ences. They were always impressed by the knowledge of this tiny slip of a woman who had been
known as "the best in the business." She said, "I'd

always take one of my old chutes along and compare it with the ones they were using. The boys would always tell me they'd never jump in anything like that! But I'd tell them it must have been okay, I'm still here!"

She was once asked how she got started jumping. She said, "To tell you the truth, I loved high places even as a child. I well remember a very tall tree in our backyard that I used to climb just to get away from everything and everybody. I could climb up into the very top and could imagine what it would be like to soar even higher."

On one of her visits to the 82nd Airborne Group at Ft. Bragg, North Carolina, she was asked if she ever had a reserve chute. She told them, "Yes, home in the garage in case I tore the one I was wearing!" She said she never used a reserve chute because she trusted the Lord, and knew that He wouldn't let anything happen to her. She added, "God has blessed me with good health and a steady nerve."

Another one of the soldiers asked her if she was scared on her first jump. She said, "Sure, I was afraid at first, for about half a minute!" She said the paratroopers couldn't believe she used simple cotton thread to mend her parachute and they said they wouldn't even jump off a lockerbox in that rig! In 1976, she was presented with the wings of the 82nd Airborne and made an honorary member of their elite group.

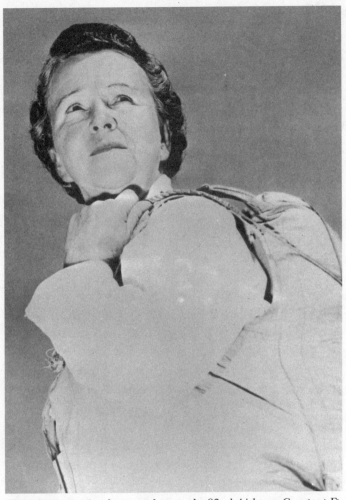

Tiny demonstrating her parachute to the 82nd Airborne Group at Ft. Bragg, North Carolina. (Courtesy of the National Air and Space Museum, Smithsonian Institution, Photo No. 2000-1372)

After the war, Tiny lived a rather uneventful life in southern California. Her work as a housekeeper made her lose contact with her old acquaintances in the aviation world, until one day when Maxine and Jim Hix came into her life. Both of the Hixes were involved with aviation and had heard of Tiny's achievements in the field. They began inviting her to various meetings of aviation groups, and in a short while Tiny was again "flying high" in the aviation world.

Maxine and Jim were responsible in large part for making Tiny famous again, and for the many honors bestowed on her. One of the first of many honors she was to receive was the United States Government Pioneer Aviation Award. She received this in 1953, on the tenth anniversary of powered flight. One of the greatest things the Hixes brought to Tiny's life was getting her involved with the many organizations that honored people in aviation. One of these organizations was the OX5 Club. Membership in this club was limited to members who were associated with the manufacture, operation, or maintenance of OX5 powered planes prior to 1941. The name was taken from the water-cooled ninety horsepower Curtiss OX5 engine, which came into being as the first aircraft power plant to be used in quantity in this country during World War I.

James Greenwood of Gates Learjet "measures"
Tiny Broadwick at the OX5 National
Reunion in Wichita, Kansas, October 1975.
(Courtesy of James R. Greenwood)

Tiny and movie star Jimmy Stewart.

Tiny Broadwick with Governor Dan K. Moore as he read a dedication to Civil Air Patrol Week in the state of North Carolina, 1968. (Courtesy of T.H. Pearce)

Tiny was given the John Glenn Medal by this group in 1964. The Director of the National Air Museum, Philip Hopkins, in presenting the medal said, "This award is for achievement in the genesis of history and Tiny Broadwick, by her achievement has written a brilliant chapter in the history of flight." He added that holding this testimonial dinner for Tiny in North Carolina was appropriate, since it was from North Carolina soil sixty years before that the Wright brothers had made their historic flight.

In 1976, Tiny was inducted into the OX5 Hall of Fame along with Charles Lindbergh, Glenn Martin, and Wilbur and Orville Wright. Tiny said, "I feel very humble and grateful for this honor. It's something I never expected!"

Another group the Hixes introduced Tiny to was the Adventurer's Club of Los Angeles. It was founded by thirty-four men in New York City in 1912 and was dedicated "to adventure, the shadow of every red-blooded man, to the game, to every lost trail, lost cause, and lost comrade, and twenty gentlemen adventurers." Their membership was limited to two hundred and there were rigid requirements for admission to their ranks. Only those who had had unusual adventures on land, at sea, or in the air; hunting, trapping, exploring, flying, or those who had attained a distinctive reputation in the field of arts, music, or science were considered eligible for membership. Not only was Tiny accepted into their club, but she was also presented in 1972 with their prestigious award of Gold Wings to signify her one thousand parachute jumps.

Of all the clubs Tiny joined however, the one she was most proud of was The Early Birds of Aviation. One of the requirements for membership in this organization was that one had to have flown solo before December 17, 1916, thirteen years to the day after the Wright brothers' first flight at Kitty Hawk, North Carolina, and until Tiny was recommended for membership, it was limited to males only.

There was some dispute about allowing Tiny to join their group. Her supporters, however, pointed out that in order to be a pioneer parachutist, Tiny was obliged to go aloft in a balloon each time she made a parachute jump; and twice she made ascents *and* descents in a balloon without using the parachute. On one occasion, the balloon was on fire and she was afraid to jump from it, and another time she was unable to detach her parachute and came down from the balloon from a height of about fifteen hundred feet. Tiny justified her eligibility for membership by saying, "I went up in the parachute and nobody brought me down!" After much discussion, she was admitted to the club, the only woman in this elite group of eighty men! She was not only given her checkerboard cap, the emblem of membership which she wore with pride, but life membership in the group as well!

Another honor accorded Tiny was her listing in Who's Who in the World of Aviation. She was also entered in the Guinness Book of World Records as the first person to perform a "premeditated freefall," and the first woman to parachute from a plane into the water. Tiny also appeared on several television shows, among which were the *Today Show* and *I've Got A Secret*.

In attending meetings of the Aerospace Club in Los Angeles, Tiny was introduced to many famous people, including Jimmy Doolittle, Omar Bradley, and astronauts Buzz Aldrin and Alan Shepard.

In 1970, one of the great moments for Tiny was being invited to witness the Apollo 13 launch at the John F. Kennedy Space Center in Florida. She said, "If I were younger, I'd be one of the first to sign up." She was once asked if she was a women's liberationist, and she was quick to answer, "Yes, I am! Believe me, when I started out, women all had to stay home. They said back home that I'd get killed. They also said the Wright brothers couldn't fly, but I've lived to see all this advancement. I just hope I live until they get ladies on the moon, and I wish I were a little girl again because I would be among the first women to go to the moon!"

Tiny with General Omar Bradley.

Tiny with famed pilot Jimmy Doolittle.

On another occasion, Tiny got to ride in the Goodyear blimp and when she was eighty-one years old, in a sailplane at Edwards Air Force Base. The pilot of the plane was Paul Bikle, former director of NASA's Flight Research Center. In 1975, she had a flight in a Lear jet and in a helicopter that she was particularly interested in. Sometimes she would take commercial flights back to North Carolina, but she said, "Current air travel is dull and unexciting. The only thrilling part of modern flying is when the plane hits an air pocket and tosses you around!"

At the time Tiny first began jumping, there was little mention of it in her hometown of Henderson, North Carolina, since joining a circus in those days was something considered unfit for a young lady to do. As a result, Tiny felt uncomfortable when she would return home because she thought that the local people looked down on her. She said, "I can go back now and if somebody snubs me, that's the old-timers. You're never respected once you make a mistake with those people. They pin you down and they never forget it. It's true. What I lived and what I've seen is real life and there's no camouflage in it. I have held on to respect and God has taken care of me."

On January 20, 1961, she was honored in her hometown however, when Mayor Carroll Singleton

Tiny is shown here with Harry Combs and James Greenwood of Gates Learjet before her flight in 1975. (Courtesy of James R. Greenwood)

proclaimed "Tiny Broadwick Day" in Henderson. How happy she must have been to have this honor and to have her hometown folks feel pride in her accomplishments.

Three years later, in 1964, Governor Terry Sanford proclaimed "Tiny Broadwick Day" in the state of North Carolina! A banquet was held in her honor in Raleigh at which time she presented one of her early parachutes to the state of North Carolina where it would be put on display in the Museum of History. She presented a second one to the Smithsonian Institute in Washington, D.C.

Another honor accorded her in her hometown was being chosen a "Hidden Heroine" by the Girl Scouts of Vance County. This was part of a nation-wide movement to honor women who had not been recognized for their service to the nation. In Tiny's honor, the scouts planted a crepe myrtle tree at the Pines of Carolina Girl Scout Council Office.

In 1982, her memory was honored in Raleigh again in the observance of "Women's Week," at which time a display of her memorabilia was unveiled at the North Carolina Museum of History.

Even though Tiny regretted having to leave her little daughter, Verla, to go with the circus, she was very pleased with the way her mother raised the child and she said, "I've talked to God many times about the care my mother took of my daughter.

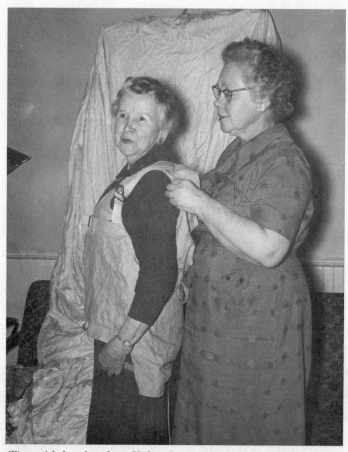

Tiny with her daughter, Verla, showing that she could still get into the Broadwick coat pack. (Courtesy of T.H. Pearce)

She's a lovely woman, she's got a lovely family, and I thank God for that!" By the time Tiny was in her seventies, she had six grandchildren, twelve great-grandchildren, and two great-great grandchildren.

In 1974, one of the greatest thrills of Tiny's life was seeing her twenty-two-year-old granddaughter, Bonnie Young, make her first parachute jump at the Franklin County Sport Parachute Center. Her eyes fairly sparkled with excitement and pride as she watched Bonnie carry on the tradition she had started back in 1908. She applauded her efforts, but couldn't help but laugh when Bonnie landed in a tree.

Though she didn't live to see it, in 1996, five other members of her family jumped to honor their grandmother since it had been such a part of her life. All of them, dressed in matching tee shirts with Tiny's name on them, wanted to experience firsthand what it must have been like for Tiny more than eighty years before. They were her grandson, Carlton, great-grandson, Rodney, her great grand-daughter, Tempe, her great grandson, Ashton, and her great-great grandson, Derek. Derek said after his jump that he might not have done it if it hadn't been for his great-great grandmother, Tiny!

There have been several attempts to rename the Henderson-Oxford Airport for Tiny because of her outstanding work in promoting the air industry.

The requests were denied however, since the officials in charge of the airport stated that they did not approve of naming an airport for an individual. Many people in Henderson feel however, that not only the airport should bear her name, but that there should also be a historic marker placed there in her honor and that her face should be put on a United States postage stamp, all of which pale in comparison to her accomplishments. Although she hasn't received this kind of recognition in her own hometown, there is a street named for her in her adopted city of Los Angeles!

In the early seventies, Tiny tried to move back to North Carolina to live out her days, but the bonds she had forged in California were too great and after a few months, she moved back to Long Beach to be with her friends.

Tiny Broadwick had a profound faith in God, and friends who knew her best say that she always carried her Bible with her wherever she went. Many of her quotes give God the credit for her accomplishments. She once said, "I do believe in God. I've been guided by Him all my life. You're never alone, you know, when you have Him. I think that's why I loved parachute dropping so much, because of that nearness to God. It's so peaceful up there with Him. And I know I'm in God's hands and if I die, you'll know where I am. I'll be better off there

(Courtesy of James R. Greenwood)

with God and I'm not afraid to go. I've had a good life and if I had my life to live over, I would do it exactly the same way."

When Tiny's dear friend, Maxine Hix, who knew Tiny better than most people did, was asked to describe her, she said, "Tiny was one of the most charming women I've ever met. She was a precious friend and a great lady. Everybody loved Tiny. She had friends everywhere. She was America's sweetheart!"

Tiny Broadwick died at the age of eighty-five on August 25, 1978, in California, but she lived long enough to know that her achievements in aviation had written a brilliant chapter in the history of flight, with over eleven hundred jumps to her credit. She was brought back home to North Carolina and laid to rest in Sunset Gardens in Henderson. Appropriately, she went home "in style," with her good friends, the illustrious Golden Knights parachuting team from Ft. Bragg, serving as her pallbearers.

With raw courage, Tiny Broadwick showed that human flight could indeed be safe. In her way, she helped give confidence to the thousands of flyers who came after her, knowing that there was a way to escape a failing aircraft if it became necessary to do so. As Philip Hopkins said, "She was small in size, but in courage she was a giant! Her contributions to flight history helped make America

Tiny with her friend Maxine Hix. (Courtesy of Dixie Young)

Tiny with members of the army's Golden Knights Parachute Team from Ft. Bragg, North Carolina. Some of this group later served as pallbearers at her funeral. (Courtesy of T.H. Pearce)

stand tall, as the nation which gave wings to the world."

Tiny paved the way for others to follow and was truly a pioneer. She will always be remembered as "The First Lady of Parachuting."

THE EARLY BIRDS

[Incorporated in the District
of Columbia, not for profit]

APPLICATION FOR MEMBERSHIP

To the Membership Committee: Baloonist

The Undersigned ~~Files~~ hereby makes application for membership in THE EARLY BIRDS and agrees that, if found eligible and worthy, he will conform to the usages, customs and rules of the organization. ~~He~~ She further states that:

Her ~~His~~ nationality is ...... American .... ~~He received membership papers~~

on .... near Oxford, Granville County,
(Strike out portion not applicable) .... North Carolina ......

Her ~~He~~ was born on .. April 8, 1893 ...... at ....

~~His~~ present occupation is .... Housekeeper and driver ....

He is connected with .... in the capacity of ....

His work in aeronautics began .... at ....

He first soloed on .. Monday, Dec.28,1908 .. at .. Jacksonville, Fla. ....

in a .... baloon .... and holds

Aero Club of .... Certificate No. ....

and he continued as follows:
(Give chronicle of experience and achievements.)

Further references to experience and achievements may be found in the following publications or records:
(References to magazines, periodicals, newspapers, papers, etc. with dates, are of interest.)

The Evening Metropolis, Dec.28,1908, Jacksonville,Fla.(Ostrich Farm)
The ALBANY Herald, (N Y) Dec.17, 1909

In submitting this application, the undersigned certifies as to its accuracy and truthfulness and that he has personally signed his full name thereto.

Date .. July 17, 1952 .... ~~Signed~~ *Tiny Broadwick* (Signature.)

Residence .. 8402 West Fourth St., Los Angeles -48-Calif. ....
Business address ..... same ....
(Print out.)

WE, the undersigned members of THE EARLY BIRDS, vouch for the good character and eligibility of the applicant and recommend his admission.

Proposer *Glenn L. Martin*

Seconder *Edward Unger*

Should it be inconvenient for the applicant to secure two members to sign this application, he may furnish three references who can vouch for him.

Name *Will D. Parker* .... Address *Butteville Okla*

X Name *John K. (Tex) LaGrone* X Address *Municipal Airport KC mo*

Name .... Address ....

Membership dues must accompany this application blank.   Dues enclosed $ ....

To: Tiny Broadwick,
A Real Aerospace Pioneer —

Alan Shepard
Bob Overmyer

Paul Weitz
Owen Garriott   Vance Brand   Tom Stafford
Bob Crippen
Gordon Fullerton   Evans
Don Peterson   Ron
Joe Engle
Bruce McCandless
Jack Swigert

Deke Slayton
Ed Mitchell
Buzz Aldrin

BIBLIOGRAPHY

Books:

Greenwood, James R. *The Parachute: From Balloons to Skydiving.* N.Y. : E.P. Dutton & Company Inc.,1964.

Hatfield, D.D. *Pioneers of Aviation.* Inglewood, Calif. : Northrop University Press, 1976.

Smith, Margaret. *North Carolina Women Making History.* Chapel Hill, N.C. : The University of North Carolina Press, 1999.

Smith, Vi. *From Jennies to Jets: The Aviation History of Orange County.* Fullerton: Sultana Press, 1985

Vesey, George and George C. Dade. *Getting Off the Ground.* N.Y. : E.P. Dutton & Co.,1979.

History of Vance County, Vol. I. Winston Salem, N.C. :

Vance County Historical Society (George T.
Blackburn II, General Chairman) and Hunter
Publishing Company, 1984.

Articles:

Goerch, Carl. "She Made Over 1,100 Jumps." *The
State Magazine* (December l, 1945).
Pearce, T. H. "First to Jump." *The State Magazine*
(January 1975).
Sitton, Gretchen. "Petticoats and Parachutes."
Women in Sports (April 1976)
Sky Diver: The International Magazine of Parachuting
(April, May, June 1973).

Newspapers:

Aerial Age Weekly . . . . July 12, 1915
The Barnstormer. . . . . Spring 1974,
    Spring 1975
The Buffalo Courier . . . . September 4,
    1913
Buffalo Evening News. . . . . September 5,
    1913
Chicago Tribune. . . . . August 17, 1913
The Daily Dispatch . . . . July 28, 1996
Dayton Daily News 1911
The Dunn Dispatch . . . . November 20,
    1974
Durham Morning Herald . . . . March 1, 1964,

March 6, 1964, November 1, 1974, November
19, 1974, March 20, 1972, January 9, 1955

Durham Morning News. . . . .   March 20, 1972

The Evening Metropolis . . . . December 28,
1908

The Florida Times-Union. . . . . January 4, 1909

The Franklin Times . . . . November 12,
1974

General Aviation News . . . . August 2, 1976

Henderson Daily Dispatch. . . . . December 18,
1976, November 20, 1974

Illustrated World . . . . September 12,
1915

Independent Press-Telegram . . . . . . February 1, 1976

Ledger Gazette . . . . March 31, 1976

Los Angeles Examiner . . . . March 9, 1915,
June 21, 1913

Los Angeles Herald Examiner. . . . . . August 3, 1974

Los Angeles Times . . . . February 10,
1914, January 10, 1914, October 14, 1966

Martin Mercury. . . . . January 4, 1946

Oxford Public Ledger. . . . . October 28,
1974

The Pilot. . . . . October 13, 1988

Pittsburgh Press . . . . June 4, 1976

The Post Intelligencer . . . . July 31, 1916

Press Telegram . . . . January 13, 1941

The Raleigh News and Observer . . . . November 25,
1974

The Raleigh Times . . . . January 13, 1961
    March 8, 1982
The San Diego Union . . . . March 9, 1914
The Seabag . . . . June 29, 1972
Southern California
    Industrial News . . . . December 30,
        1968
The State: South Carolina's
    Progressive Newspaper . . . . December 29,
        1946
Sunday Tribune . . . . March 22, 1913
Valley Times. . . . . October 13,
    1953
The Washington Post . . . . October 13,
    1988
The Wichita Sunday Eagle
    and Beacon . . . . October 20,
        1975

Interviews:

Greenwood, James R.
Hix, Maxine
McLean, Lyman
McPolin, Father Pat
Pearce, T.H.
Young, Dixie

Index